IDEAS IN P

Castration

Ivan Ward

Series editor: Ivan Ward

ICON BOOKS UK

TOTEM BOOKS USA

Published in the UK in 2003
by Icon Books Ltd., Grange Road,
Duxford, Cambridge CB2 4QF
E-mail: info@iconbooks.co.uk
www.iconbooks.co.uk

Published in the USA in 2003
by Totem Books
Inquiries to: Icon Books Ltd.,
Grange Road, Duxford
Cambridge CB2 4QF, UK

Sold in the UK, Europe, South Africa
and Asia by Faber and Faber Ltd.,
3 Queen Square, London WC1N 3AU
or their agents

Distributed to the trade in the USA
by National Book Network Inc.,
4720 Boston Way, Lanham,
Maryland 20706

Distributed in the UK, Europe,
South Africa and Asia by
Macmillan Distribution Ltd.,
Houndmills, Basingstoke RG21 6XS

Distributed in Canada by
Penguin Books Canada,
10 Alcorn Avenue, Suite 300,
Toronto, Ontario M4V 3B2

Published in Australia in 2003
by Allen & Unwin Pty. Ltd.,
PO Box 8500, 83 Alexander Street,
Crows Nest, NSW 2065

ISBN 1 84046 442 9

Series editor: Ivan Ward

Typesetting by Hands Fotoset

Printed and bound in the UK by
Cox & Wyman Ltd., Reading

Introduction: The Castration Complex Defined

The castration complex is a constellation of childhood beliefs and emotions that pertain to the dawning awareness of a fixed sexual identity. These include, for the boy-child, a belief that the mother once had a penis, that it was cut off by the father or a father substitute, and that his own sexual organ may be subject to the same gruesome fate.[1] Emotions range from the initial refusal to believe such a preposterous idea, through outraged defiance, to acute anxiety and eventual capitulation. Like the Oedipus complex, the effects of castration anxiety are woven into the fabric of life in a unique way for each person, and how a child deals with the castration idea has profound implications for his or her future. It may be denied, displaced, projected, sexualised, or turned round upon the self. For the girl-child there is the additional belief that she herself once possessed a penis that has been brutally and unjustly removed. The repercussions of this imaginary castration may be acute feelings of loss, or a disturbing sense that the body has been damaged.

3

Using examples from everyday life and commonplace cultural references, this book examines:

- the importance of the concept in Freud's work
- the symptomatic reality it explains
- its paradoxical role in child development
- the mechanisms through which it achieves its effects
- its function in human sexuality and love
- its influence on creativity and creative inhibition, and
- the ethical concerns it illuminates

Castration and Beginnings

Freud wrote of castration in his 'Little Hans' case history of 1909,[2] and first used the term 'castration complex' in his paper 'On the Sexual Theories of Children' (1908).[3] It was out of the mouths of children that he chose to give birth to his most controversial and unbelievable concept.

In the last decade of Freud's life, castration anxiety loomed more and more into prominence; it began to swallow up the other anxieties and 'danger-situations' of *separation, loss of love*, and *death*, which he had established as the cornerstone of psychoanalysis in 1926, and which seemed, in comparison, so common-sensical.[4] By the time of his last major work, the castration complex had almost fused with the Oedipus complex and was of equal importance.

'[U]nder the influence of the castration complex', Freud writes, the boy-child 'experiences the severest trauma of his young life.' He continues:

The results of the threat of castration are multi-farious and incalculable; they affect the whole of a boy's relations with his father and mother and subsequently with men and women in general.[5]

The Oedipus complex was once described as the 'emotional attitudes' a child has to its parents and siblings;[6] now those relationships are themselves motivated and organised by the castration complex. 'The whole occurrence', says Freud, 'may probably be regarded as the central experience of the years of childhood.'[7]

A Note on Explanation: Castration and the Black Hole

But what kind of 'central experience' can it be which is completely forgotten? 'The whole occurrence …', Freud continues, '… is so completely forgotten that its reconstruction during the work of analysis is met in adults by the most decided disbelief. Indeed, aversion to it is so great that people try to silence any mention of the proscribed subject and the most obvious reminders of it are overlooked by a strange intellectual blindness.'[8]

Freud is routinely lambasted for positing bizarre invisible entities and offering untestable, magical explanations, so it may be valuable to introduce an analogy from a 'hard(er)' science. How can one study an entity which is the psychical equivalent of an astronomer's black hole?

Firstly we can study its effects in surrounding fields of experience. If the castration complex is as important as Freud claims it is, then its gravitational pull should distort mental space and affect the distribution of mental objects. The black hole in space may inhibit the movement of a nearby star, or speed it up; throw it off course or obscure its existence. Similarly, inhibitions or over-excitement, loss of mental balance or the absence of mental capacities may be investigated as possible effects of the castration complex. Melanie Klein showed how inhibitions at school could be related directly to the 'dread of castration'. What appeared to teachers as laziness or lack of interest, or awkwardness in games and athletics, revealed itself to Klein as a 'neurotic inhibition' and a child buckling under the weight of castration fears. It was as if the child said: 'If I do X, I will be punished (by castration).' (e.g. 'If I do something which symbolically represents my desire for mother, I will be punished by castration.') Only when the castration anxiety was resolved was it possible to make progress with the inhibition. Similarly, a person's special interests and sublimations may be a means of escape from the spectre of castration. For thirteen-year-old Felix, sex and football had became entwined in phantasy. 'Coitus had already been replaced by football', Klein recounts, 'and had absorbed his interest and ambition entirely.'[9] The football was 'a protection against other repressed and inhibited interests less consonant with the ego';[10] that is to say, those interests which bring with them the danger of attack.

Secondly we can investigate the black hole from first principles. If you have a gravitational pull X, a critical mass Y, and atomic nuclei with the characteristics Z, then you will end up with an object so massive and compact that light cannot escape. In similar fashion, a woman on a Channel 4 television programme hypothesised from first principles about castration. She remembered a male friend who compulsively touched his crotch whenever he spoke excitedly among his friends. 'It must be strange having such a sensitive organ on the outside', she noted, 'I'd be worried about it getting snapped off or bitten by a dog.'[11] Any mother (or girlfriend) knows that the penis is of intense interest to the little boy who owns it. She may also be aware of her own complex feelings towards it. In ancient times, phallic symbols and amulets were worn or touched to protect the owner from danger.[12] From first principles, then, we might say that such a psychically significant and precious object will inevitably bring with it the possibility of loss. Thus when the time is right, according to Freud, it takes very little to activate a sense of threat. There is, one might say, a *preconception* of castration in the mind; it seems to arise inevitably from within.[13]

Considering the third way in which the castration complex can be investigated, analogies with the astronomer break down. A black hole does not exist because the universe has the *idea* of a black hole, yet the 'castration complex' is very much a matter of beliefs. One day, four-year-old Daniel told me of a curious implement he had heard about at the Anna Freud Centre nursery. It was called a 'willy-cut'. A willy-cut was like a pair of garden shears but with a much more restricted range of functions. After enquiring how he came to such a notion it transpired that he had based his sense of conviction on slender evidence; he had over-heard one of the therapists at the centre utter the enigmatic word – 'Winnicott'!

In days when psychoanalysts used their own lives as part of the data of analytic investigation, E. Pickworth Farrow described his reaction after uncovering the memory of a brutal castration threat, believed by him to be real: 'For some days the writer was utterly miserable, and felt himself back in the time when he was a small helpless child expecting his genitals to be clipped off the next moment', he writes, 'and he never felt so completely lonely and lost in the world before.'[14]

Symptomatic Reality and Castration: Hallucination

The despondency which accompanies castration beliefs is reason enough to banish such thoughts from awareness. Despite this, we can sometimes see castration ideas and castration fears revealed directly in adults. Like a Leviathan rising from the deep, they can come to terrorise the conscious mind and dominate a clinical picture. As a child, Freud's Russian patient, known as the 'Wolf Man', rejected the possibility of castration only to be overwhelmed by the hallucinated vision of his severed finger hanging from a thread of skin. Such was also the case with Daniel Paul Schreber, a distinguished Appeal Court Judge in Germany, who became perhaps the most famous patient in the history of

psychiatry. Schreber's fame rests on the publi-
cation of his *Memoirs of My Nervous Illness* in
1903 which he compiled from diary entries and
notes kept during a nine-year confinement at
various psychiatric clinics and asylums in
Leipzig and Dresden. Freud's analysis of this
'invaluable book' secured its place in the history
of psychoanalysis.

The *Memoirs* is a work of personal religion
and philosophy, designed to answer some of the
riddles of Schreber's tragic existence and to
explain himself to his wife and family. It was
also a work of vindication, proving the reality of
'what other people think are delusions and
hallucinations'. Like all great stories, Schreber's
book describes a journey. From a withdrawn
state of virtual catatonia, overwhelmed with
anxiety, massively deluded and tortured by
gruesome hallucinations about his body and his
surroundings (the so-called 'miracles'), Schreber
slowly begins to make sense of the catastrophe
that has befallen him and resume contact with
the outside world. In a beautifully evocative
passage, he describes the pivotal moment of
insight:

The month of November 1895 marks an important time in the history of my life and in particular in my own ideas of the possible shaping of my future. I remember the period distinctly; it coincided with a number of beautiful autumn days when there was a heavy morning mist on the Elbe. During that time the signs of a transformation into a woman became so marked on my body, that I could no longer ignore the imminent goal at which the whole development was aiming.[15]

From this moment, Schreber could build another kind of reality from the ruins of his previous mental existence. In order to escape some other 'horrible end', he reconciles himself to the thought of being transformed into a woman.[16]

There were still supernatural elements intent on changing his attitude back again – or 'forsaking' him. Malicious 'rays' would make 'hypocritical appeals' to his 'sense of manly honour' and taunt him with sarcastic insults: 'Are you not ashamed in front of your wife?', or, still more vulgarly: 'Fancy a person who was a *Senatsprasident* allowing himself to be f----d.'

Schreber remained undaunted and steadfast in his mission:

However repellent these voices, however often I had occasion to air my just indignation in one way or another during the thousand-fold repetition of these phrases, I did not allow myself to be diverted from that behaviour which I had come to recognise as essential and curative for all parties – myself and the rays.[17]

In this way, Schreber side-steps the unspeakable horror of castration. He is no longer faced with the prospect of being a castrated male but a 'spirited woman' destined for great things. In the final life-affirming elaboration of the delusion, he was to be impregnated by God for the purpose of creating a new race of human beings. Schreber, who at one time was forced to pretend to be a corpse, had become the saviour of mankind. From that moment of insight he began to live again.

I would like to meet a man, who, faced with a choice of either becoming a demented human

*being in male habitus or a spirited woman,
would not prefer the latter.*[18]

Perhaps a similar mental leap could have rescued
a less famous patient from the tragic impact of
castration hallucinations, described to me some
years ago. Found hanging in his garage one
evening after supper, none of his family realised
that he had been tormented for years by the
feeling that his penis was continually being cut
off and attached to other parts of his body.[19]

Psychoanalyst Samuel Ritvo writes of a similar
case in which hallucination is ameliorated and
replaced by fantasy:

*He suffered intense, conscious castration anxiety,
fantasising himself the victim of accidental or
intentional castration many times a day.*[20]

This person did not imagine, as others may do,
that the dog across the street would run towards
him and bite his hand, or that he might fall off a
ladder and break his leg. Rather the dog would
sink its teeth into his penis and as he fell from
the ladder his genitals would catch something

and be ripped from his body. It was as if all his other symptoms – anxiety attacks, nausea, anorexia, abdominal cramps, phobic and obsessional symptoms – were an efflorescence of the core castration threat. The history of such individuals reveals a concatenation of early traumas and disturbed relationships. Repeated somatic illnesses, early separations, disturbed or neurotic parents (anxious, aggressive or depressed), all contribute to the severity of castration fears and the inability to surmount them. In the grip of a morbid anxiety from which few of us are entirely free, here was a man living precariously on the edge.

Child Development and Castration: Childhood Memories

Childhood memories do not only recall the past, but symbolically represent it. Leonardo da Vinci remembered a strange incident from his childhood. He was lying in his crib when a bird of prey flew down and 'opened my mouth with its tail, and struck me many times with its tail against my lips'.[21] In his psychobiography of the artist, Freud interpreted the story as a manifestation of the castration complex. Similarly surreal childhood memories were recounted recently on the BBC radio programme 'Desert Island Discs', in which distinguished guests are invited to reminisce about their lives and select the eight favourite records they would take to an imaginary desert island.

The record which the much admired actor Timothy Spall associated with the first memory was 'New Fangled Tango', sung by Lena Horne. It is a song full of sexual suggestiveness and innuendo, about a new kind of dance in which 'you don't need steps'.

When I was young the front room of the house was always locked and kept for special occasions. I used to break in to play my mother's records.[22]

The second story, with its disarming 'I was a bit of a hypochondriac' and 'I had an active imagination', speaks of nightmarish fears about the body which few of us are able to escape.

I was a bit of a hypochondriac. A man used to

walk by the house with a big nose and someone said he had his nose made from his bum because he had cancer of the nose. Because I had an active imagination I used to think I had a pain in the nose and I'd have to have my bum put on my nose.[23]

The last tale develops a classic scenario of teenage horror, the monster in the attic.[24]

My grandmother lived on the top floor of the house. She used to love gorgonzola cheese, and kept it in a dish in her room. It looked as if it was rotting. My brother and I used to sneak into her room and lift the lid off the cheese dish. We'd go 'Uurgh!', look frightened, and run away.[25]

With its foetid smell and veins of blue mould, one is hardly surprised if Gorgonzola cheese could also acquire the significance of rotting flesh. That's what the young thespian seemed to see at any rate.

Taken together, the three memories form a single thematic narrative. A story of temptation, transgression, punishment and suffering. The young boy enters the forbidden maternal space and is threatened with a mutilating punishment. The prospect brings forth a vision of putrefying flesh and he is thrown into a kind of purgatory, compelled to gaze upon the horror of his imagining. In Freud's developmental narrative, the memory (the *screen* memory) echoes and replaces an earlier moment. In the grip of his cocksure Oedipal strivings, the little boy discovers that the mother long regarded as identical to him is lacking the most revered aspect of his identity.

Like most of us, Timothy Spall remembers his childhood terrors with amused nostalgia. Freud took such memories and injected the emotion back into them: each moment, each fleeting image, each narrative twist took on the weight of a momentous childhood experience. These are the 'unmistakable reminders' of castration anxiety he talks about: the revolting sight of a lump of cheese or the terror of an itchy nose.

Child Development and Castration: Growing Up

Here's a puzzle. What do these incidents have in common?

1 Bertie the dog waits panting with expectation while Jack the toddler holds onto his ball. Adults nearby are unable to persuade him to throw the ball for Bertie.

2 Chris Carson's property developer father accuses him of having an overactive imagination and tells him it is time he grew up. He helps his son along by ripping up the drawings that testify to the boy's continuing belief in ghosts.

3 Religio-political fanatics fly a plane into the World Trade Center buildings and the Pentagon. Commentators call the horrific events a 'wakeup call' for the American nation.

Each of these incidents tells us something about the ordinary difficulties of growing up. In growing up, we relinquish part of our narcissism. We give up certain objects, beliefs, and modes of gratification. Infantile megalomania and phantasies of self-sufficiency are shattered. We are obliged to realise that there are *other people in the world*, and *they are not all like me*.

In a few weeks, Jack will be driving his mother to distraction by throwing things from his buggy and expecting her to retrieve them. But for now it is Jack's ball and he is not giving it up without a struggle. The ball feels part of him, and his main impulse may be to put it into his own mouth. Under the benign gaze of the grown-ups, he stands in a developmental no-man's land looking puzzled and distressed: put the ball in his mouth, or throw it in order to play?

Of course, being Hollywood, Casper the ghost soon becomes Dad's best friend as well, and together they save Chris from being blown up in the house which dad was trying to demolish. Growing up, for Chris, required negotiating something physically intimidating and dangerous.

The destruction wrought by the attacks of September 11 was routinely interpreted through the metaphor of 'growing up', as if the attack on these symbols of power – the Twin Towers, the Pentagon building, the Capitol – somehow reso-nated with the losses we experience as children.

For Freud, these inevitable traumas form a series, including 'castration', and anchor them-selves in specific bodily functions. Many parents have experienced the delicate task of negotiating the separation of at least one valued bodily object.[26] 'Bye bye, pooh' I used to say with my daughter as we waved it into the toilet. August Starke added 'nipple' to the series through a supposition that the baby at first regards the mother's breast as its own possession (much like the baby's mother may regard him or her).[27] When the nipple proves to have a life of its own, the baby experiences the first great blow to its narcissism. Klein lays stress on this early trauma and the convulsive rage and splitting that results. Intent on holding onto his narcissistic delusion, the world is split into good and bad; the *good breast* inside me always, and the hated *bad breast* 'out there'. Thus growth of the personality takes place not only through the loving attention of adoring parents but also through an unavoidable succession of traumatic ruptures and losses.

Three things result from this process of traumatic loss: (1) and this most often spoken of, the setting up of a fantasied object inside the mind which takes the place of the lost object in the outside world, (2) an emotional scar, more or less severe, upon which future growth is accomplished, and (3) a knot of anxiety at the core of one's being.

A fourth outcome is the increased emotional and structural complexity of the mind. As development proceeds, a symbiotic relationship with the mother is transformed into a three-person relationship,[28] described by the French psychoanalyst Jacques Lacan as a movement from the 'Imaginary' to the 'Symbolic' realm,[29] or by Mary Target and Peter Fonagy as a process of 'triadification'.[30] The co-ordinates of mental space are transformed. Mother-figure and father-figure get drawn into the formation of the superego:

A precipitate in the ego consisting of these two identifications in some way united with each other.[31]

Yet despite this genealogy, the superego 'retains the character of the father'.[32] Forged in the white heat of the castration threat, the superego is now saddled with the task of repressing the impossibly intense emotions of the Oedipal drama. Clearly no easy task, as Freud puts it.[33] It is the father-figure as obstacle and prohibition on Oedipal desires which imparts its character to the superego. That is to say, the father as the perceived agent of castration.[34] In order to become a socially responsible person, disencumbered of his narcissistic delusions, the child is fated to accept the reality of castration. And it is the life-threatening impact of this possibility, as far as the child is concerned, which ushers in the momentous transformations of this period.

Freud was aware that his schematic descriptions could provide only the scaffolding upon which a life of flesh and blood is built. So many factors are involved in the process; different qualities of attachment to mother and father, different constitutional propensities, different degrees of actual intimidation or parental seduction. It is impossible to predict how things will eventually turn out. A child's personality may be crushed by the weight of too severe castration anxiety, or become uncontained and uncontrollable. Whether the person will become homosexual or heterosexual, active or passive, fearful or independent, controlled or uninhibited, depends on the play of a multitude of forces. Yet through it all, the castration complex and its effects are a constant factor, acting as a pivot between past and future. In his book *Paranoia*, also published in this series, David Bell quotes Freud's grammar of homosexual desire. Taking the kernel sentence 'I (a man) love him (a man)', Freud shows an array of possible outcomes: erotomania ('I do not love him, I love her'); pathological jealousy ('I do not love him, *she* loves him'); and homophobia ('I do not love him, I hate him', leading inexorably to the paranoid 'He hates me'). Each transformation pivots around the impact of the threat of castration, yet depending on the play of forces and chance events which push development one way or another, opposite behaviours may result.

The castration fantasies which plagued Ritvo's patient above were formed in the context of his disturbed family relationships. Castration fears in their turn determined aspects of his current relationships and attitudes to men and women. Thus the absent father of his infancy, whose reappearance must have been so unwelcome to the patient, becomes under the threat of terrible retribution the idealised figure of a friend with whom he compares himself in later life. The seductive mother on the other hand, at one time a source of temptation and sensual pleasure, becomes the most feared creature – a woman – 'physically strange and repulsive, genitally mutilated, controlling, and demanding'.[35] The castration complex transforms the emotional tone of relationships. Psychical values are realigned so that good becomes bad or pleasure becomes pain. Through the retrospective process of free association, psychoanalysts uncover the deeply buried ideas and fantasies of castration, and the path taken in life to avoid awareness of them. Thus Jean Laplanche and J.-B. Pontalis in their acclaimed dictionary of psychoanalysis can say with little fear of contradiction from their colleagues: 'The castration complex is met with constantly in analytic experience.'[36]

Child Development and Castration: Playing With Reality

'Whereas it is easy to see that children play for pleasure', suggested Donald Winnicott, 'it is much more difficult for people to see that children play to master anxiety, or to master ideas and impulses that lead to anxiety if they are not in control.'[37] He might also have added that children play to help them grow up, or in some cases to help them *not* grow up.

As a young man, cyclist Lance Armstrong used to play a game. He would soak a tennis ball in kerosene, light it, and play 'catch'. Describing this story, Kalu Singh compares young Armstrong to Prometheus, the Titan who defied the lightning bolts of Zeus to bring fire down to earth. Such was his adolescent hubris, his trainer Chris Carmichael observed, '*He just thought he was King Shit.*' But the castration threat will not be denied. One day he felt something metallic in his throat. Suddenly he was confronted with an unmistakable reminder of his mere mortality. 'And not just mere', as Singh says, 'but at the core of masculinity, in those very balls of fire and life, testicular cancer.' Yet it was only after his experience of cancer that he was able to realise the potential of his prodigious athleticism. 'Before Lance had cancer', explained Carmichael, 'we argued all the time. He never trained right. He would do what you asked for two weeks, then flake off and do his own thing for a month or two.' The treatment required a different kind of fire: and the chemotherapy was so intense it left burns on his skin *from the inside out*. Yet Armstrong rose from the fires, fighting to be more than fit. And he rose from the flames transformed. No longer chained to the rock of illusory self-sufficiency, he began to follow the instructions of his trainer and work together with his team. Out of the renunciation of his heroic independence, he achieved a different order of mental functioning and became one of the immortals to win the *Tour de France* four times in succession.

Lance Armstrong's adolescent game would have been quite normal in a four-year-old. At least the structure and function of the game, if not its specific content. Just as Freud's eighteen-month-old grandson threw a cotton reel from his cot in order to master the trauma of the mother's disappearance,[38] so the three- or four-year-old symbolically recreates the threat of castration in his games and phantasies, and triumphs over the danger. Miriam found as much when she went to babysit young Sam and came back shell-shocked.

'He's got a game that he makes me play over and over again', she said, 'It's called the crocodile game.'

'And how does it go?' I ask.

'I've got to be a crocodile, then I have to chase him and he runs away. And then he turns round and starts "killing" me.'

'And what would the crocodile do if it catches him?'

'I don't know, but he says it has something to do with bottoms.'

Her jaundiced view of the irritating child was moderated on the next occasion she saw him. The anxiety infusing the game was revealed in all its heart-rending poignancy as he woke in abject terror in the middle of the night screaming for his mother. The wearisome little monster was suddenly revealed as the vulnerable and frightened child he always was, desperately attempting to control his inner fears and impulses.

Child Development and Castration: Pleasure

In a story of thwarted desire, writer Auberon Waugh remembers his father soon after the war sitting down in front of the anguished eyes of his children and eating the entire ration of bananas which Waugh and his sisters knew to be 'the most delicious taste in the world'. Recounting the story in his autobiography, Waugh concludes:

It would be absurd to say that I never forgave him, but he was permanently marked down in my estimation from that moment in ways which no amount of sexual transgression would have achieved.

From that moment I never treated anything he had to say on faith or morals very seriously.[39]

A sense of justice and injustice is forged in the furnace of family life, including the child's inevitable ideas of 'the privileges and prerogatives with which the parent is felt to be endowed'.[40] The incidental reference to 'sexual transgression' indicates the currents of feeling contained in the story. It is about the envied and feared father keeping all good things for himself, and exclusive access to a source of pleasure which can only seem grossly unfair to the boy whose passions are so intense. Would he never experience such pleasure himself?

Some analysts have taken the capacity for

pleasure as a central factor in castration. Freud's biographer and disciple Ernest Jones, in rejecting what he called the 'phallo-centric' bias of the castration idea, coined the term 'aphanisis' to indicate the complete abolition of the capacity for sexual enjoyment. Rather than the 'central experience' of childhood, castration was only an aspect of this more general fear which applies equally to men and women.

Despite these admirable democratic intentions, Jones undermines his argument by citing the case of an obsessional young man. 'He had substituted the idea of aesthetic enjoyment for that of sexual gratification', writes Jones, 'and his castration fears took the form of apprehension lest he should lose his capacity for this enjoyment, *behind them being of course the concrete idea of loss of the penis.*'[41]

Jones is the first to admit that the unconscious does not deal in abstractions, and in the stories we have heard so far it is the concrete, imagistic language which gives them their impact – bananas and cream, bums and big noses, mouldy gorgonzola. To turn Jones on his head, we could say that he has discovered one facet of castration fear, but one among many. If castration means a loss of sensual pleasure, it is also a loss of self-esteem. It is also a loss of the capacity to symbolically reunite with the figure of the mother, and finally a loss of the ability to make babies (potency) – a fear which can be transferred onto other forms of creativity. Perhaps in any individual, one or other of these capacities will be regarded as most significant and castration fear will be skewed in that direction. Some men are willing to undergo a surgical procedure which increases the size of their flaccid penis at the cost of its erectile function. It is not the loss of sensual pleasure they fear but the loss of the penis as an object of narcissistic display. My father, trapped in a life-threatening situation during the Second World War, experienced what he called a 'divine anger' which obliterated all fear from his mind. His indignation against the Almighty (father) was encapsulated in the thought that *he would never have children*.

Child Development and Castration: Sexuality

The confluence of *pleasure* and *identity* with the

demands of the *social world* is what makes human sexuality puzzling and unique. Castration is fundamental to four aspects of sexuality: the acceptance of sexual difference; the denial of sexual difference; the production of sexual excitement; and as a cause of sexual inhibition.

Freud sometimes speaks of sexual identity as if it is a question of choice. You can want *this* or you can want *that*, you can put yourself in this position or that position. It appears a matter of choice because sexual identity is formed in the context of sexual difference, our relations to male and female, mother and father; a field of possibilities.

'The Oedipus Complex offered the child two possibilities of satisfaction', wrote Freud, 'an active one and a passive one ... He could put himself in his father's place ... or he might want to take the place of his mother and be loved by his father.'[42]

Much of the early analytic debates about sexual difference (often centred on the problem of 'female sexuality') boil down to a simple question: 'are the sexes born or made?'[43] How each protagonist to the debate answers this question determines in part their attitude to the importance of castration. If you are in the 'born' camp, then castration anxiety becomes an unfortunate experience that you may or may not come across in childhood, like measles or chicken pox. If you are in the 'made' camp, then castration is the unavoidable precondition for your sexual identity, the hidden hand that makes you choose one path rather than another. Whatever inherent differences there may be between boy-babies and girl-babies, by emphasising the bisexual disposition of each sex, the active and passive aims of each sexual drive, and the inherent ambivalence of all human relationships, Freud clearly puts himself in the 'made' camp.

The Parisian psychoanalyst Joyce McDougall recounts a charming story about her four-year-old grandson, Daniel. Enquiring intensely about his mother's pregnancy during the day, he was eager to benefit from his new-found knowledge when his father returned from work in the evening. 'Daddy, I've got something special to ask you. Would you please put a baby in my tummy too?'[44]

McDougall speaks of a 'primary homo-sexuality' to emphasise the bisexual possibilities of early childhood and the attendant fantasies of eating, penetrating and possessing parents of the same sex, while wishing to *become* the parent of the opposite sex and 'incarnate all the privileges and prerogatives with which that parent is felt to be endowed'.[45] But the fool's paradise is not to last. Aggression and envy complicate the picture, confused feelings of guilt and the fear of narcissistic injury. 'Eventually all children must accept the fact that they will never possess both genders and will forever be only half of the sexual constellation', says McDougall, a circumstance she describes as 'a scandalous affront to infantile megalomania'.[46]

The child's discovery of the difference between the sexes is matched in traumatic quality by the earlier discovery of otherness and the later revelation of the inevitability of death. Some individuals never resolve any of these universal traumas, and all of us deny them to some degree in the deeper recesses of our minds – where we are blessedly free to be omnipotent, bisexual, and immortal![47]

For Freud, who sees infantile bisexual longings extending well into the Oedipal period, the closing down of these possibilities comes about through the threat of castration. Castration becomes a symbol of sexual difference, and negotiating the castration threat determines the assumption of one identity rather than another. We 'choose' our sexual identity by finding the path of least resistance around the black hole of castration. Clearly no easy task.

Joyce McDougall's pioneering work on 'neo-sexualities' has shown in detail how her patients *come to terms* with this universal dilemma in a perverse way, having 'short-circuited the elaboration of phallic-oedipal anxiety'.[48] In her view it is damage done to the body image in the pre-Oedipal relation (creating a body as alienated, fragile, mutilated, devoid of eroticism) which pushes development towards the perverse solution. That is to say, a perverse solution to the problem of castration.

Clinical observation has convinced me that those children who are destined to acquire sexually deviant behaviours in adulthood initially created their erotic theatre as a protective attempt at self cure. Confronted with overwhelming castration anxiety stemming from Oedipal conflicts, at the same time they were faced with the need of coming to terms with the introjected image of a fragile or mutilated body.[49]

Perverse sexuality makes extensive use of pre-genital forms of excitation as a way of avoiding the castration threat ('the whole terrifying mystery of castration' as Fenichel calls it).[50] At other times, genital sexuality is preserved, but surrounded by certain conditions which must be strictly adhered to. Thus the phallic exhibition-ist, through displaying his genitals, defends against castration anxiety and assures himself that his penis is not fragile and mutilated but powerful and beautiful.[51] By focusing his sexual interest onto an object rather than a person, the fetishist disavows the existence of the female genital and the horror of castration it arouses.[52] The sadist and masochist triumph over the anxiety by inflicting and welcoming pain, inclu-ding attacks upon the genital itself.[53]

But these perverse solutions are not greatly

different from 'normal' development. Each person, according to Freud, makes some adjustment to their sexual behaviour which may be called 'perverse'. We get 'turned on' by particular items of clothing or bits of the body ('fetishism'), create fantasy scenarios, or transgress taboos (sometimes self-imposed) to spice up our love lives. No one is surprised at a shop selling S&M fashion called *Pink Piranha*, or one selling fetishistic lingerie called *Aphrodisiac*.[54] Speaking on a BBC radio programme, garden designer Susanna Walton described the Dragon tree with its red sap that oozes out like blood if the trunk is cut. With scarcely a nod in the direction of ordinary logic, she adds, 'Of course, it's been regarded as an aphrodisiac for thousands of years.' Flirting with danger and the possibility of castration-punishment is part of the ordinary process of generating sexual excitement. But there is a difference. A person dominated by perverse sexuality, like a child in the grip of overwhelming anxiety who is unable to play with freedom, constructs highly controlled, fixed repetitive rituals. He injects excitement into the body from outside, like a drug.[55] Danger generates the excitement; the motive for the ritual is not ultimately pleasure, no matter how intense it is, but the evacuation of anxiety, and emotions which would lead to anxiety if not held in check. It is about the avoidance of psychic pain and the triumph over danger.

It goes without saying that in the realm of romantic love, flirting with danger, with the threat of castration, plays a significant role. In the great love stories of history – Samson and Delilah, Tristan and Isolde, Eloise and Abelard, Lancelot and Guinevere – the theme of castration figures literally or figuratively. It is hardly a coincidence that the physical feelings of 'falling in love' are indistinguishable from the manifestations of fear, not just for our medieval forebears but for us as well. In medieval iconography, love's arrow is usually aimed at the heart or eyes. However, 'the witty illustrator of an Italian version of the *Lancelot* romance has his young hero struck by Love's arrow not in the eye but in the crotch'.[56] A coloured German woodcut by Master Caspar of Regensberg ('Frau Minne's Power Over Men's Hearts') displays

38

the brutal tortures of the lover's unfortunate organ. 'No fewer than eighteen hearts are pummelled, squeezed, sawn in half, pressed with thumb screws, and speared like so many kebabs by Frau Minne', states Camille, adding: 'The inscriptions in German refer to the power of women over men's hearts.'[57] Freud notes in 'Analysis Terminable and Interminable' that men are quite happy to develop such masochistic relations to women as a defence against the same masochism in relation to other men. In this case, the feared attacks are displaced onto the woman as a sexualisation of the anxiety. I need hardly add that the throbbing heart was frequently equated with the penis.[58]

Love only exists when there is an obstacle to love, an obstacle created by the third term of the Oedipal triangle, and one whose dire punishments are ever present in the unconscious mind of the male lover. These are the life-threatening dangers of every Hollywood blockbuster, which the hero overcomes to win his beloved. Examples are superfluous. But what of the situation for women?

La Castrata?: It's Not So Different For Girls

In an astonishing failure of nerve (astonishing because it is so unlike him) Freud argued that although women were subject to a castration *complex*, they did not experience castration *anxiety*. He made this claim (remember this was the man who created the concept of psychic reality and who delved into the most bizarre manifestations of our phantasmagorical lives) on the grounds of logic – how could the girl experience a castration threat if she felt she was already castrated? The answer is – surprisingly easily. Castration anxiety can arise either in relation to the supposed castration of the mother, or as a repetition of an imaginary trauma. When Miriam was three years old, she went into a hysterical screaming fit because her father, in giving her a slice of melon, threatened to cut off a knobbly bit of rind at the end of the slice. Her mother was called 'Melony' (Melanie). Destined to be herself the victim of the crocodile game, it took many weeks of collaborative storytelling about little monkeys chased by crocodiles before the monkey saved its tail by turning and confronting its frightening attacker. The stories acted as an emotional processor, gradually containing and moderating the anxiety.[59]

Israeli analyst M. Woolf gave an even more explicit example in 1955. A little girl growing up on a kibbutz refused to sleep in the children's house. Each time the mother tried to take her back, apparently asleep, the girl woke trembling and crying, 'The dog has bitten off my wee-wee.' The overwhelming anxiety, like a phobic reaction, which women may experience at the thought of menstruation, or sexual intercourse, or giving birth, clearly has its roots in earlier castration anxiety.[60] Fenichel describes a case in which early sexual abuse by a trusted relative contributed to a paralysing fear of castration in a woman and wide-ranging inhibitions in her sexual life.[61] How Freud could have missed the obvious indications of castration anxiety in women and its role in establishing their position within the sexual dyad is difficult to fathom. By focusing only on 'penis envy' and the depressive effects of loss (that is, the imagined loss of an imagined penis), or feelings of inferiority and shame, Freud undermined his own assumption of the importance of castration. For both sexes, castration anxiety, and how it is overcome, plays a key part in the articulation of sexuality. Likewise, Freud's infamous 'penis envy' applies equally to men and women. That is to say, envy of the magnificent penis one would *like* to have, or the idealised penis one imagines the father possesses. Castration wishes against the father, from both sexes, rebounding on the subject through the fear of retribution, are a major contribution to castration anxiety.[62]

Castration and Psychical Splitting

Something else happens under the impact of castration which is pertinent to the problem of mental structure. Just as earlier traumas create the dimensions of good and bad in relation to the mother,[63] the trauma of castration creates an irrevocable split in the figure of the father. (The castration complex also influences the later split between the affectionate and sexual attitudes to the mother, 'Madonna' and 'Whore'.[64]) For reasons which remain obscure, modern psychoanalysts rarely comment on this phenomenon, despite the obvious ambivalence of the father–

son relationship. Luckily, Hollywood has no such qualms. Chris Connor's father hires a fanatical commando to plant explosives in the house he intends to demolish. Once it is known that Chris himself is trapped in the building, his father tries to stop the bombing, only to find that his alter ego has run amok and, like the deranged pilot in *Dr. Strangelove*, refuses to follow a countermanding order. There ensues a desperate struggle between the hateful murderous father and the loving protective father which, for Chris's sake, the loving father has to win. Since it is a children's comedy, we can guess the outcome. Chris's reward for his brush with death is a kiss from the girl he has admired from afar. With Casper's help, he can win the girl *and* be reconciled to the formerly castrating father.

Similarly, in Hitchcock's espionage thriller *North by Northwest* (1959), Roger O. Thornhill ('What does the 'O' stand for?' 'Nothing') gets plunged into a nightmare world of mistaken identity and unexplained violence. The film opens with the suave advertising executive trying to keep at bay a series of demanding women, including his mother.[65] Suddenly, men are out to get him, but he does not know why. His frantic efforts to escape take place within the context of paternal splitting. Both father figures block access to the inevitable object of sexual interest, the beautiful and alluring spy Eve Kendal. The 'Professor' is Eve's spymaster and the murderous van Damm is her lover. Eve herself embodies the dual aspect of the mother, complicit in the murderous intent of the father figures at one moment, seductive and protective the next. Roger finally resolves the Oedipal dilemma by saving Eve from van Damm, who has learned her true identity, and the Professor no longer has reason to keep the two of them apart. Thus, even without a friendly ghost to help him, Roger circumvents the problem of castration and is reconciled to the 'good Father'.

Freud's work is full of such examples. The paintings of 17th-century artist Christoph Haizman present a series of images of the devil with whom he made a delusional 'pact'. The devil first comes to him 'as an honest elderly citizen with a brown beard, dressed in a red cloak and leaning with his right hand on a stick, with a black dog beside him'.[66]

This benign image was soon to change:

Later on his appearance grows more and more terrifying – more mythological, one might say. He is equipped with horns, eagle's claws and bat's wings. Finally he appears in the chapel as a flying dragon ...[67]

Not only, concludes Freud, does the figure of the devil derive directly from the father, but in the infantile unconscious of the artist, and perhaps all of us, god and the devil are one. The consequences of a psychical split between the castrating and castrated aspects of the father is one of the great unconsidered problems of psychoanalysis.

Castration and the Return of the Repressed

The sense of immediacy, perhaps, is what distinguishes the *return of the repressed* from other manifestations of the unconscious. The Wolfman, as a child, *sees* his severed finger hanging by a bloody thread and begins to faint; fictional Mafia boss Tony Soprano faints at the sight of cooked meats in order to disavow the memory of his father's butchery;[68] Dostoevsky, whose novels of murder, parricide and punishment were determined in part by the murder of his own father, suffered epileptic attacks and fits of fainting. The return of the repressed is what hits you in the gut, and is sometimes impossible to bear. In each of these cases the reaction is like a victim of torture. Some small incident in the present triggers a violent physical response because it is reinforced by an experience from the past that may be completely forgotten and unconscious.

Such was my reaction in watching the film *The Piano Teacher* (2001). I suddenly felt hot and clammy, dizzy and nauseous. A cold sweat set my skin tingling. I knew I was going to faint.

The scene which caused me to faint involved the depiction of female genital self-mutilation. The eponymous piano teacher, played by Isabelle Hupert, is a cold and controlling middle-aged woman living a claustrophobic relationship of hate and dependency with her mother. In contrast to the probity of her professional life, teaching at the conservatory, she has a secret life of solitary sexual perversion which she conducts with the same sadistic control that she inflicts on her pupils. In the scene in question she is in the bathroom at home. Her mother is about to call her for dinner. Naked, she unwraps a razor blade from a cloth, steps into the bath and sits on the rim of the bathtub. Taking a hand mirror to see more clearly between her legs she carefully cuts her genitals with the razor blade, and blood trickles down the side of the bath. The image is shot in profile so the audience do not actually see anything apart from the small trickle of blood. Why should this cause me such alarm?

You might think that's a stupid question. But once we ask it we realise that it is not so easy to say what is 'traumatic' in a trauma. It cannot be the blood – anyone who watches the ubiquitous hospital dramas on TV will see more blood. Scalpels cut into flesh in glorious technicolour and graphic close up. Neither of these images make me feel giddy and nauseous. Even scenes of castration (*In the Realm of the Senses*) or the threat of castration (*Mississippi Burning*) do not produce such an effect. It must have been something to do, not with the image, but the 'idea' of the scene. Given the theme of genital mutilation it must have been the experience of castration anxiety that rose from the unconscious to overwhelm me. But another factor is involved.

The castration complex is also a constellation of beliefs, as we have seen. A theory about sexual difference and how it came about. One of these beliefs is the idea that the mother has a penis, and Freud contended (from his study of children's sexual theories and the fantasies of his adult patients) that it is in relation to the supposed castration of the mother that the castration complex has its momentous effect on the little boy. Most people find this idea so shocking and unbelievable – perhaps I should say 'illogical' – that they forego the simple expedient of asking children themselves. It is precisely in the chasm between the child's conception and the adult's that Freud locates his concept of the unconscious.

Now we see why this scene was so powerful. It was not what it showed but what was hidden that effected the trauma. The spectator sees 'nothing'; the genitals are obscured by the woman's thigh as she sits on the rim of the bath. But out of nothing is conjured up the archaic memory of the mother-with-a-penis, and the horrifying castration that she was once thought to have suffered. This is the central knot of the castration complex in all its unbelievable absurdity, lying deep in the unconscious.

Sometimes the unconscious returns not as horror but as beauty. In the film *American Beauty* (1999), the central striking image of a young woman on a bed of rose petals may, through the common equation of body and phallus, be seen as the wish-fulfilling transformation of a much more disturbing image – a dismembered penis in a sea of blood.[69] If this idea seems unbelievably grotesque, then let me put it in more mundane terms. When a man suffers from a 'mid-life crisis', as does the dead hero of this film, it may be that there is an anxiety at the root of it which has some sexual meaning. The so-called 'male menopause' often brings in its wake the hypochondria and anxiety that we suffered from as children but have since forgotten (remember Timothy Spall's 'I was a bit of a hypochondriac').

Loss of capacities, loss of desire and the sense of impending death bring castration fears from the past into the present. In his extraordinary and moving paper 'The Theme of the Three Caskets', Freud shows through a study of myth and literature how the goddess of death, who takes us finally into her arms, may be represented by the most beautiful and lovely of women. Such is the power of illusion to triumph over reality.

Creativity and Castration: Masturbation Fantasies and Sublimation

It was probably the famous American sexologist Alfred Kinsey who said that 99% of adolescent boys masturbate and the other 1% were liars. Yet shame and secrecy still surround the practice. Why should that be so?

Judge Schreber may have accepted being impregnated by God, but he was reluctant to admit his ordinary masturbation. Such was the shame of the frightful business that he could only describe his masturbatory activity through a tortured narcissistic logic: 'male and female …

in one person ... having intercourse ... with myself'. In fact Schreber was probably right that what he did was different from ordinary masturbation. Schreber's masturbation had no need for fantasied sexual objects, whereas for the child in the throes of Oedipal passion, his masturbation is intimately connected to the content of that complex. 'As can be clearly shown', claims Freud, 'he stands in the Oedipus attitude to his parents; his masturbation is only the genital discharge of the sexual excitation belonging to the complex, and throughout his later years will owe its importance to that relationship.'[70] Once more Freud stresses the *complete* structure of the Oedipus complex in which the boy can take up either a masculine or feminine position. Each possible alternative brings its attendant dangers. (Schreber's refusal at first to adopt either position indicates the disavowal of castration that lies at the heart of his psychosis.)

Perhaps Schreber had read one of the many medical tracts warning of the dangers of self-abuse, in vogue during the late Victorian era. The precursor of these, *Onania* – or, *The*

Heinous Sin of Self-Pollution, and all its Frightful Consequences in Both Sexes, Considered – was published anonymously in 1710, probably by a quack selling bottles of tonic, but it struck a chord which could be traced way back to antiquity and across a multitude of countries and cultures. For the author of *Onania*, onanists can expect to suffer blindness, insanity, stunted growth and, eventually, death. Nearly three hundred years later, it is remarkable that teenage masturbation is still engulfed in a fog of shame and furtive anxiety, while infantile masturbation is hardly ever discussed. On learning that Princess Diana's butler was apparently dispatched to the newsagents to procure 'wank mags' for her sons, novelist Howard Jacobson lamented what the boys were missing by having the butler do the shopping:

No listening to the libido as it shapes its promptings, no mustering of the forces of resistance, no argument between the Jekyll and the Hyde of one's sexual nature, which argument Jekyll will always lose, but only after the libido has flooded the whole system with those chemicals to which we give the simple name of desire, but which in fact also encompasses self-loathing and self-destruction and insanity.[71]

Could it be that the centuries old war on masturbation, and the puzzling sense of 'sin' attached to it, is not a simple conspiracy of church or state, but an index of a danger at the heart of sexual expression itself?

Freud puts it thus:

When the (male) child's interest turns to his genitals he betrays the fact by manipulating them frequently; and he then finds that the adults do not approve of this behaviour. More or less plainly, more or less brutally, a threat is pronounced that this part of him which he values so highly will be taken away from him. Usually it is from women that the threat emanates; very often they seek to strengthen their authority by a reference to the father or doctor, who, so they say, will carry out the punishment ... Now it is my view that what brings about the destruction of the child's phallic genital organisation is this threat of castration. Not immediately, it is true, and not without other influences being brought to bear as well.[72]

So what happens to all that manic energy? What happens to the tidal wave of emotion?

The libidinal trends belonging to the Oedipus complex are in part desexualised and sublimated … and in part inhibited in their aim and changed into impulses of affection. The whole process has, on the one hand, preserved the genital organ – has averted the danger of its loss – and, on the other, has paralysed it – has removed its function. This process ushers in the latency period, which now interrupts the child's sexual development.[73]

You go to school. Learn to read. You find something to do that binds the energy, modulates the inchoate urges and phantasies, attenuates the anxiety. Something repetitive is good, something that occupies the hands or inhibits their function. Boys spend hours kicking a ball from foot to foot to keep it from the ground, or shooting demons and monsters in video games.

Cricket genius Don Bradman found such an activity in his youth. He would spend countless hours of solitary practice hitting a ball against the garden wall of his family home in New South Wales, making the task more difficult for himself by hitting a *golf* ball with a cricket *stump*. Bradman's repetitive ritual, like my own and countless others' at the same age, was a substitute for masturbation. Or rather, it was a 'compromise formation'. It is a surrogate masturbation activity, but it also embodies the prohibition against masturbation; it expresses aggression and it controls aggression; it enacts a phantasy of triumph and 'transcendence', with the exhilaration and joy of passing each milestone of ritual achievement, while it expresses submission to reality as represented by 'the laws of nature'. In engaging in a socially acceptable activity, the child controls both the inner world of dangerous temptation and the outer world of paternal disapproval. As Freud might put it – the libidinal currents are 'tamed' and diverted in their course. Embodied in these simple repetitive acts are the sublimated fears and desires of a latency-aged child. And even if we cannot predict their final outcome, in their unconscious meaning lies the deep well of emotion from which can spring future greatness. In contrast to the agitated ritual of his youth, Bradman's mature batting technique was characterised by an almost Buddha-like stillness when facing the bowler.

In another field altogether, comedian Billy Connolly found a calming influence in his troubled young life when he took up playing the banjo:

Something about the playing of this instrument, perhaps the regular strumming and repetition of phrases, was surprisingly soothing for him. From then on, he and his banjo could barely be prised apart.[74]

His wife and biographer Pamela Stephenson is not so enamoured. She recounts a typical family argument in which the symbolic meaning of the instrument and the anxiety it evades is not far from the surface.

'What's the difference between a banjo and an onion?' I tease him. 'Nobody cries when you slice up a banjo.' ...

'How many banjo players does it take to change a lightbulb?' he returns. *'Just one, but he does it over and over again.'*[75]

It is probably no surprise to discover that in one of his legendary stage performances, Connolly treats his audience to a graphic masterclass in advanced masturbation:

'The opening line is all-important', explains Billy. *'Say "Thank God you're here!"'*[76]

Creativity and Castration: Light and Knowing

Bathed in a circle of light, Connolly rushes round the stage like a man possessed, 'strutting, striding, tilting at windmills',[77] yet finding a kind of beatific peace out there in the spotlight.

'Ironically' says his wife *'Billy's earliest memory is one of being terrified by a circle of light'* ... *'Until he was three years old, he and his beloved sister Florence slept in a curtained-off alcove in the kitchen. One evening she aimed a mirror*

reflection onto the wall, allowing it to pirouette and chase him until he screamed for mercy.'[78]

Pamela Stephenson does not tell us what was so frightening to the three-year-old child. But we know. Like its sister, blindness, the theme of light is a common one in the spectacle of castration. In turning the castrating, piercing light of his childhood into the warm blanket of light that surrounds him onstage, Billy Connolly has triumphed over the infantile dread through a supreme creative act. Like Schreber but without the hallucinations.

When Lance Armstrong played fireball, he probably didn't connect his ball of fire to the celestial fireball that passes across our heads each day. The myths of antiquity show sun-gods as a masculine principle, both castrated and castrating – the Egyptian Ra or Greek Uranus. One of Melanie Klein's child patients, John, burnt bits of paper in the consulting room, and cut up a yellow pencil with a knife. 'The yellow pencil stood for the sun', Klein interprets, and 'had a further significance as his father's sadistic penis.'[79] In an extraordinary twist, the most insubstantial object of our experience – light – comes to represent what might seem to many the essence of masculine substance – the father's phallus. Thus, when Tristan is mortally wounded for his sexual transgression and returns to his homeland in Brittany, his abject state is represented in Wagner's opera by the incessantly scorching sun that beats down on him. Or consider Isaac Newton. As a young boy, he too played a kind of fireball. He tied fireworks to a home-made kite which he flew at night in stormy weather to frighten people below. He wanted them to think it was a comet crashing down to earth. Like Einstein after him and Leonardo before him, he was fascinated with light. It was Newton who realised that the solid beam of light which he allowed into his darkened room was not a single entity but composed of all the beautiful (feminine?) colours of the rainbow. In this act of genius, Newton completed his own Oedipal triumph. He had cut up the father's phallus into pieces. One might imagine that the eccentric genius would have enjoyed the acclaim this work brought him. Instead he retreated to his room for ten years, working on problems of alchemy and poring over biblical texts to prove the doctrine of Unitarianism, that God was not a Trinity but an indivisible entity. Having destroyed the father, he spent the next ten years trying to put him back together again. A story of hate, guilt and reparation that was only finally resolved when Newton reconciled the laws of the universe – that is to say, the laws of God to man – in his magnum opus, the *Principia Mathematica*. It is said that he never had another creative thought for the rest of his life.

Creativity: 'Grown Up' Art and Castration

For both Klein and Freud, the problem of *creativity* is connected to the problem of *inhibition*. Felix was a whiz on the sports field but a dullard in the classroom; Leonardo's passion was painting, but he left only a handful of masterworks. A similar confluence can be seen in the work of contemporary artist Damien Hirst.

Art allows us to see the world in a different way and produces objects of 'beauty' or wonder. By this measure, Damien Hirst is undoubtedly an important artist. Yet there is something deeply uncreative about his work. Often Hirst merely copies objects he has seen in the outside world and makes them bigger. 'Spot paintings' like Sigmar Polke painted thirty years earlier; 'Spin paintings' like the ones you can make with the children's 'Swirl Art' sets from Woolworth's; his majestic twenty-foot statue 'Hymn' – an exact replica of an anatomical toy found in the Science Museum shop. Despite his genius, it is as if the dangers of more elaborate creative thinking are too great.

In his most controversial work, we find reason for his creative inhibition. 'Mother and Child Divided', a cow and calf sawn in half and placed in four tanks of formaldehyde, is a symbolic enactment of brutal separation between mother and child. Like Leonardo, whose *Madonna and Child with St Anne and John the Baptist* depicts a similar doubling of mother and child, Hirst experienced a particular kind of attachment and separation from his own mother in the first few years of his life. Hirst was born in secrecy in Bristol, the father did not want to know, and it was a year before his mother moved back to her home city of Leeds. When Damien was about two or three years old, she met someone and got married.

Hirst's Turner-prize-winning installation reflects something of this story. It is not an abstract contemplation of life and death, nor a simple desire to shock, but evidence of an emotional being trying to make sense of itself, trying to represent, or be represented. 'Mother and Child Divided' echoes the process of division the little child felt when this new man appeared on the scene: his anguished feelings of betrayal; the anxiety and foreboding; his impotent rage and fervent wish to divide this new man from his mother. It re-enacts a traumatic moment and changes it. Because it is no longer Damien Hirst who feels the rupturing effects of the process, rather it is he who, in the act of destruction and creation, now takes the place of the father and his imaginary role. Damien Hirst is now the one with the chainsaw, and he invites the spectator to join him in the carnage. We walk through the tanks of formaldehyde with their grizzly contents as if repeating the process of division, implicated in the drama as spectators.

It is through the fear of castration that the father has his inhibiting effect, not only the castration one fears for oneself but the genital mutilation one imagines for the mother. In another work, 'Forms without Life', Hirst displays large polished seashells mounted in display cabinets on the wall. Contemplating the piece in the Tate Modern art gallery, my ten-year-old daughter questioned its artistic value: 'It's not very creative is it? All he's had to do is go into a shop and buy some beautiful things and put them on the wall.' Under the weight of castration anxiety, the female genital, often compared to the shells of sea creatures, becomes a 'Form without Life' since the truly living part of it (as far as the little boy is concerned) has been removed. In this work, Damien Hirst is stuck at this point. Unable to engage or 'play with' the symbolic connection between sea shell and vagina, he is (or was) unable to imbue new life into the objects which, as my daughter observed, have simply been transposed from a shop to a gallery. As Melanie Klein said all those years ago, creativity is inhibited by the 'dread of castration'.

Ethics and Castration: Moral Outrage

Freud relates the trait of defiance not only to the anal phase of the 'terrible twos', but also, as we have seen, to defiance of the castration threat. The English longbow-men at Agincourt stuck two fingers up at their French enemies because the fingers would be cut off if they were captured. Nobody likes losing a finger, but it is the symbolic meaning of the act which turns this gesture into the 'Fuck you!' of male defiance. Clearly this 'masculine protest'[80] is not the only basis of moral outrage. However, a strenuous reaction against castration is a significant contribution to much of the anger we see displayed around us by individuals and groups.

Someone who has taken moral outrage to an art form is Billy Connolly himself. His live performances abundantly confirm John Cleese's contention that comedy is a form of 'revenge'. They are peppered with attacks on the irrational, the mendacious, the pompous and the spiteful. Phrases like 'Can ya believe it!' and 'It's an AB-SO-LUTE disgrace!' typify his style and attitude, as he whips himself up into a frenzy of indignation. Performances can go on for more than three hours – the stage persona somehow taking over the real Billy Connolly, and not letting go.

Born into poverty, abandoned by his mother, beaten by his carers, abused by his father, Billy's life sounds like a catalogue of woe. His comic routines synthesise and modulate the traumas of his life, gaining symbolic mastery over that which mastered him. Castration is never far from the surface. Billy, whose recent British TV series ends with him riding off, naked, on his motorcycle, and whose on-stage masturbation has already been mentioned, started his exhibitionist tendencies early. A little after the frightening incident with the light beam, the defiance kicks in. Having been refused a desired piece of cake, he threatens the neighbour, Mattie, looking after him: 'Then I'll touch you with my chookie', he threatens, and begins to unbutton his flies. 'But, after catching sight of Mattie's horrified face', writes Pamela Stephenson, 'he ran round and pinched her bottom instead.' On another occasion, Billy urinates in the street and deliberately sprays the backs of girls sitting on the pavement.[81] His defiant, extravagant behaviour disavows the threat of castration – sticking two fingers up to fate.

Ethics and Castration: The Problem of Guilt

In some castration myths it may appear that castration is the desired result of the story and that what underlies it is a profound envy of women's creativity. Egypt's solar god Ra castrated himself to bring forth a race called the Ammiu out of his blood. The phallus of the Hindu 'Great god' Mahadeva was removed and chopped to pieces by priestesses of the great goddess. The pieces entered the earth and gave birth to a new race of men, the Lingajas (men of the *lingam*, or phallus). In Mexico, the Aztec god Quetzalcoatl made new humans to repopulate the earth after the flood by cutting his penis and giving blood to the lady of the serpent skirt – a goddess with many short phalli dangling about her waist. The Babylonian god Bel voluntarily cut off his 'head' (= penis) and mixed his blood with clay to make men and animals. The sky-god Uranus was castrated by his son Cronus. Uranus's severed genitals fell into the sea and fertilised it to produce a new incarnation of the Virgin Aphrodite. It was she who ruled cults of castrated gods, such as Anchises and Adonis.[82] A recent archaeological discovery in North Yorkshire, sensationally reported in the *Independent* newspaper ('Pagan Transvestite Priest Died After Ritual Castration'), showed the burial of a priest of an important Roman religious cult devoted to the sun-god Attis and the mother-goddess Cybele. The cult's priests would ritually castrate themselves in solidarity with Attis, and dress in women's clothing.[83] Even Tertullian admitted that the 'divine mysteries' of Christianity were similar to the 'devilish mysteries' of pagan saviours like Attis, and the popularity of Attis's cult in Rome led to Christian adoption of some of the older god's ways.[84] In comparing early medieval images of the infant Christ with the crucifixion image, the castration theme is clear. The genitals disappear in the crucifixion image and are replaced by a bloody wound. If the unconscious does indeed work by the law of talion, we can only assume that the sin which Christ is redeeming his brothers for is not only killing the primal father, as Freud proposed, but also castrating him. If I add 'and eating his penis', it is not to try to persuade you to believe something fantastical, but because the practice of eating the penis of one's enemy has not been rare in the history of mankind. It is expressly *forbidden* in the book of Genesis (Genesis 32:32).

These myths attest to men's attempt to undermine the notion of women's creativity. It is now the disembodied phallus which becomes the fount of creativity and the social order.[85] In cases of self-castration, which predated the early Christian church but which seem somehow so suited to the Christian ethos, the holy intention was to eliminate sin and temptations of the flesh. In fact self-castration can be a holy purpose in social groups in which women are regarded as the most debased and evil of creatures. One can only assume that the 'temptations' prohibited by the Almighty raised the prospect of a castration much more frightening than the one self-administered. Thus guilt may not only be a consequence of the dread of castration, but real or symbolic self-castration may be a profound solution to the problem of Oedipal guilt.

Ethics and Castration: Redemption

Exhibiting a tiger shark in a glass tank, Damien Hirst represented in unmistakable terms the castrating father who cannot be avoided. In calling it 'The Physical Impossibility of Death in the Mind of Someone Living', he suggests that the primitive image of the father does not die. Something in this emotional landscape is frozen – petrified we might say. The child's image of the terrible father, thought by Freud to be genetically determined but reinforced or moderated by the emotional sensitivity or thoughtlessness of parents, casts a chilling shadow over the rest of his life.

In a recent production of Richard Wagner's music drama *Parsifal* at Covent Garden, a stuffed shark hovered above Klingsor's magic garden in Act 2, much to the amusement of audiences and indignation of critics. Perhaps the producers noticed a central theme in Wagner's work and decided that a shark was an appropriate object to symbolise it.

For those who do not know the story, Klingsor is the evil sorcerer out to destroy the knights who guard the Holy Grail and their leader Amfortas. Klingsor is evil, but he once wanted to be good; so he castrated himself. Another character tells the story in Act 1:

Unable to kill the sinful, raging lust within him, his hand upon himself he turned ...

That act of self-mutilation gave Klingsor magical powers, and with them he produced a magic garden in the desert, full of beautiful women who would lure the good knights away. Amfortas tried to defeat Klingsor. But it turned out he was not so good after all. He was seduced by Kundry, a complex female character who is both Klingsor's chief temptress and, in another guise, seeking forgiveness, a helper of the Grail Knights. Klingsor stabs Amfortas with his own spear, leaving a gaping wound in his side that would never heal.

Before Parsifal can accomplish his holy mission of saving Amfortas and restoring the Knights of the Grail to their former glory (potency), he has to confront the threat which Klingsor repre-sents and overcome it. Klingsor's sin is not made explicit in the drama, but Parsifal's temptation is crystal clear. It is overcoming incestuous longings that is the task Wagner gives Parsifal as the redeemer in the story. Kundry attempts to seduce Parsifal by drawing him into his forgotten past, evoking Gamuret, his long-dead father, and Herzeleide, his over-protective mother who brought him up alone.

Of love now learn the rapture
that Gamuret once learned,
when Herzeleide's passion
within him fiercely burned!
For love that gave you
life and being,
must death and folly both remove,
love send
you now
a mother's blessing, greets a son
with love's first kiss!

So Parsifal, who grew up in ignorance of this Oedipal dynamic (as did the other great 'idiotic' Wagner hero, Siegfried), is now forced to bring his incestuous desires in line with both a mother *and* father. He is not slow in learning the consequences. Kundry leans over him 'and presses her lips to his mouth in a long kiss', as Wagner's stage directions say.

Suddenly Parsifal starts up with a gesture of intense fear; his demeanour expresses some fearful change; he presses his hands tightly against his heart, as though to subdue a rending pain.

'Amfortas!
The Wound! The Wound!'

At the moment of incestuous temptation it is the image of castration that bursts through into his consciousness. But paradoxically it is the repudiation of sexuality which allows sexuality to come into being. Experiencing the incestuous temptation and confronting the threat of castration – going through the experience as it were – allows entry into the promise of a sexual life with non-incestuous sexual partners and identification with the father. Soon Parsifal himself will become a father. He redeems Amfortas by healing his wound with the magical spear, and takes his place.

Wagner's opera symbolises aspects of the inner world and unconscious processes. If it is legitimate to leap from art to politics, it might be argued that the ideology of national redemption which crystallised in Germany during the inter-war period gave the same mental impulses a terrifying reality.[86]

Castration and the End

When the women of Greenham Common pinned baby clothes onto the perimeter fence of the Cruise missile base and chanted 'Take the toys from the boys', they expressed a truth about male activity and the phallic insecurity that underpins it. The impulse to redemption and towards reconciliation with the castrating (and castrated) father is another unconscious reason for masculine activity. It is one of the most profound feelings a man can experience, often most intense at the birth of his own son. After the first Hydrogen bomb was exploded in November 1952, bringing the energy of the sun down to earth, physicist Edward Teller wrote a short exuberant telegram to Los Alamos: 'It's a boy!'[87]

The castration complex is: a set of infantile beliefs; a developmental moment; a phylogenetic inheritance; an organiser of sexual difference; a key determinant of a person's character and destiny. The effects of the castration complex are wide ranging and incalculable, for the individual and for culture. Through its role in the formation of the superego, the castration complex helps explain why the horrors of humanity spring from the same source as our highest ideals. As far as this book is concerned, it barely scratches the surface.

Acknowledgements

Thanks to Kalu Singh for his creative input and friendly support.

Notes

Throughout the Notes, SE refers to the *Standard Edition of the Complete Psychological Works of Sigmund Freud*, trans. J. Strachey, London: Hogarth Press, 1953–75.

1. In Freud's view, childhood castration fantasies refer to the *penis* rather than the testicles, whose sexual significance is at that time unknown.

2. Freud, S., 'Little Hans' (1909), SE 10.

3. Freud, S., 'On the Sexual Theories of Children' (1908), SE 9.

4. Freud, S., *Inhibitions, Symptoms and Anxiety* (1926), SE 20.

5. Freud, S., *An Outline of Psychoanalysis* (1938), SE 23, p. 190.

6. Freud, S., 'Preface to Reik's *Ritual: Psychoanalytic Studies*' (1919), SE 17, p. 261.

7. Freud, S., *An Outline of Psychoanalysis*, op. cit., p. 191.

8. Ibid., p. 191.

9. Klein, M., 'Early Analysis' (1925), in *Love, Guilt and Reparation*, Delta Books, 1975, p. 90.

10. Ibid., p. 91.

11. 'A Man's Best Friend', prod. and dir. D. Doganis, Channel 4, 7 October 2002.

12. Mattelaer, J., *The Phallus in Art and Culture*, Pub. European Association of Urology (no date found).

13. Bion, W., 'A Theory of Thinking' (1962), in *Second Thoughts*, New York: Jason Arundsen, 1967.

14. Pickworth Farrow, E., 'A Castration Complex', *International Journal of Psychoanalysis*, vol. 6, 1925, pp. 45–53.

15. Schreber, D.P., *Memoirs of My Nervous Illness* (1903), trans. and ed. I. Macalpine and R. Hunter, London: William Dawson and Sons Ltd., 1955, chapter XIII.

16. Ibid., p. 148.

17. Ibid., p. 148.

18. Ibid., p. 149.

19. Creighton, F., personal communication.

20. Ritvo, S., 'Anxiety, Symptom Formation and Ego Autonomy', *Psychoanalytic Study of the Child*, vol. 36, 1981, p. 341.

21. Freud, S., 'Leonardo da Vinci and a Memory of his Childhood' (1910), SE 11, p. 82.

22. Interview with Timothy Spall, 'Desert Island Discs', BBC Radio 4. (Not exact quotations.)

23. Ibid.

24. See Ward, I., 'Adolescent Phantasies and the Horror Film', *British Journal of Psychoanalysis*, vol. 13, no. 2, pp. 267–76.

25. Interview with Timothy Spall, op. cit.

26. Freud, S., 'On Transformations of Instinct as Exemplified in Anal-erotism' (1917), SE 17, pp. 127–33.

27. Starke, A., 'The Castration Complex', *International Journal of Psychoanalysis*, vol. 2, 1921, p. 179.

28. Young, R., *Oedipus Complex*, Cambridge: Icon Books, 2001.

29. Lacan, J., and Granoff, W., 'Fetishism: The Symbolic, the Imaginary and the Real', in Lorand, S., and Balint, M. (eds), *Perversions, Psychodynamics and Therapy*, New York: Gramercy Books, 1956.

30. Target, M., and Fonagy, P., 'Fathers in Modern Psychoanalysis and Society: The Role of the Father and Child Development', in Trowell, J., and Etchegoyen, A. (eds), *The Importance of Fathers: A Psychoanalytic Re-evaluation*, London: Routledge, 2002.

31. Freud, S., 'The Ego and the Id' (1923), SE 19, p. 34. See also Roth, P., *The Superego*, Cambridge: Icon Books, 2001.

32. Freud, S., 'The Ego and the Id', op. cit., p. 34.

33. Ibid., p. 34.

34. See Davids, F., 'Fathers in the Internal World', in Trowell, J., and Etchegoyen, A. (eds), *The Importance of Fathers*, op. cit.

35. Ritvo, S., 'Anxiety, Symptom Formation and Ego Autonomy', op. cit., p. 341.

36. Laplanche, J., and Pontalis, J.-B., *The Language of Psychoanalysis*, trans. D. Nicholson-Smith, Hogarth Press, 1973, p. 57.

37. Winnicott, D.W., *The Child, the Family, and the Outside World*, Harmondsworth: Penguin Books, 1964, p. 144.

38. Freud, S., 'Beyond the Pleasure Principle' (1921), SE 21.

39. Waugh, A., *Will this do?* (1980), Carroll and Graf, 1998.

40. McDougall, J., *The Many Faces of Eros*, London: Free Association Books, 1995, p. xii.

41. Jones, E., 'The Early Development of Female Sexuality' (1927), in *Papers on Psychoanalysis*, London: Balilliere, Tindall and Cox, 1948, p. 440, my emphasis; reprinted Karnac Books, 1997.

42. Freud, S., 'The Dissolution of the Oedipus Complex' (1924), SE 19, p. 176.

43. See Leader, D., 'The Gender Question', in *Freud's Footnotes*, London: Faber and Faber, 1999, pp. 120–52.

44. McDougall, J., *The Many Faces of Eros: A Psychoanalytic Exploration of Human Sexuality*, London: Free Association Books, 1995.

45. Ibid., p. xii.

46. Ibid., p. xiv.

47. Ibid., p. xv.

48. Ibid., p. 182.

49. Ibid., p. 181.

50. Fenichel, O., 'The Psychology of Transvestitism'

(1930), *The Collected Papers of Otto Fenichel* (First Series), New York: Norton and Co., 1953.

51. Kahr, B., *Exhibitionism*, Cambridge: Icon Books, 2001, pp. 46–8.

52. Pajaczkowska, C., *Perversion*, Cambridge: Icon Books, 2000, pp. 36–7.

53. Welldon, E., *Sadomasochism*, Cambridge: Icon Books, 2002.

54. See Steele, V., *Fetishism: Fashion, Sex and Power*, Oxford: Oxford University Press, 1996.

55. Abel-Hirsch, N., *Eros*, Cambridge: Icon Books, 2002.

56. Camille, M., *The Mediaeval Art of Love: Objects and Subjects of Desire*, New York: Harry N. Abrams Inc., 1998, p. 40.

57. Ibid., p. 117.

58. Ibid., p. 112.

59. See Music, G., *Affect and Emotion*, Cambridge: Icon Books, 2001, pp. 23–4.

60. Woolf, M., 'Castration Anxiety', trans. S. Kut, *International Journal of Psychoanalysis*, vol. 36, 1955, pp. 95–104.

61. Fenichel, O., 'Introjection and the Castration Complex' (1925), in *Collected Papers*, vol. 1, New York: Norton and Co., 1953.

62. Alexander, F., 'The Castration Complex in the Formation of Character', *International Journal of Psychoanalysis*, vol. 4, 1924, pp. 11–42.

63. See Bell, D., *Paranoia*, Cambridge: Icon Books, 2002.

64. See Freud, S., 'A Special Type of Object Choice Made By Men' (1910), *Contributions to the Psychology of Love 1*, SE 11.

65. Through a process of projection, 'demanding' = 'castrating'. In Freud's world, being unable to 'commit' is being unable to negotiate the castration anxieties which

such commitment would entail. Much easier to cope with a woman's demands than the fearful consequences of one's own.

66. Freud, S., 'A Seventeenth-Century Demonological Neurosis' (1923), SE 19, p. 85.

67. Ibid.

68. Welldon, E., *Sadomasochism*, op. cit.

69. Lewin, B., 'The Body as Phallus', *Psychoanalytic Quarterly*, vol. 2, 1933, pp. 24–47.

70. Freud, S., 'The Dissolution of the Oedipus Complex', op. cit., p. 176.

71. Jacobson, H., 'It's the Furtive Shame That Makes a Boy a Man', *The Independent*, Saturday 9 November 2002.

72. Freud, S., 'The Dissolution of the Oedipus Complex', op. cit., pp. 174, 176, 177.

73. Ibid., p. 177.

74. Stephenson, P., *Billy*, HarperCollins, 2002, p. 136.

75. Ibid., p. 140.

76. Ibid., p. 56.

77. Ibid., p. 6.

78. Ibid., p. 7.

79. Klein, M., 'A Contribution to the Theory of Intellectual Inhibition' (1931), *Love, Guilt and Reparation and Other Works 1921–1945*, New York: Delta, 1975.

80. Alfred Adler's felicitous expression is discussed by Freud in Freud, S., 'Analysis Terminable and Interminable' (1937), SE 23, p. 250.

81. Stephenson, P., *Billy*, op. cit., pp. 22–3.

82. From Walker, B.G., *The Women's Encyclopaedia of Myths and Secrets*, 1983; adapted by K. Taylor at http://www.geocities.com/WestHollywood/Village/3025/castrate.html.

83. 'Pagan Transvestite Priest Died After Ritual Castration', *The Independent*, Wednesday 22 May 2002.

84. Walker, B.G., *The Women's Encyclopaedia of Myths and Secrets*, op. cit.

85. The horrific genital mutilations which mark the rites of passage of young men and women in some societies (I won't describe them here) are not about feminisation as such, but symbolic negotiations of castration as part of the process of taking one's place within the sexual dyad. The old stamp their authority on the young and bind them to the social order through pain.

86. Theweleit, K., *Male Fantasies*, Oxford: Polity/Blackwells, 1987.

87. Easlea, B., *Fathering the Unthinkable: Masculinity, Scientists and the Nuclear Arms Race*, London: Pluto Press, 1983, p. 130.

In case of difficulty in obtaining any Icon title through normal channels, books can be purchased through BOOKPOST.

Tel: +44 (0)1624 836000
Fax: +44 (0)1624 837033
e-mail: bookshop@enterprise.net
www.bookpost.co.uk

Please quote 'Ref: Faber' when placing your order.

If you require further assistance, please contact:
info@iconbooks.co.uk